# Tess in a Mess

by Holly Harper

illustrated by Tom Jellett

It is Tess and Ross.

Sit on the
rug, Tess.

Tess ran on the rug.

Mud on the socks!

Tess gets in a mess.

Pull on
the rocket!

Ross gets the mug.

Tip in the red packet.

Dip it into
the mug.

Peg it up, Ross.

Encourage students to use the pictures to retell the story.